D0907089

My Farm

My Horses

By Heather Miller

Children's Press
A Division of Grolier Publishing
New York / London / Hong Kong / Sydney
Danbury, Connecticut

Special thanks to the Unger-Finks at Condee Farm in Davie, Florida

Photo Credits: Cover and all photos by Angela Booth

Contributing Editor: Jennifer Ceaser
Book Design: MaryJane Wojciechowski

Visit Children's Press on the Internet at:
http://publishing.grolier.com

Library of Congress Cataloging-in-Publication Data

Miller, Heather.
  My horses / by Heather Miller.
    p. cm. — (My farm)
  Includes bibliographical references and index.
  Summary: A young girl describes how she cares for a mother horse and colt.
  ISBN 0-516-23108-1 (lib. bdg.) — ISBN 0-516-23033-6 (pbk.)
  1. Horses—Juvenile literature. 2. Horsemanship—Juvenile literature. [1. Horses.] I.
Title.
SF302.M52 2000
                                     636.1'083—dc21
                                     00-020922

Contents

My name is Nikki.

I have some good friends.

I run to meet my friends
after school.

5

My friends are my horses.

One of my friends is big.

My other friend is smaller.

This is my horse, Star.

Star is a **mare**.

A mare is a mother horse.

This is Coco.

Coco is a **colt**.

A colt is a young horse.

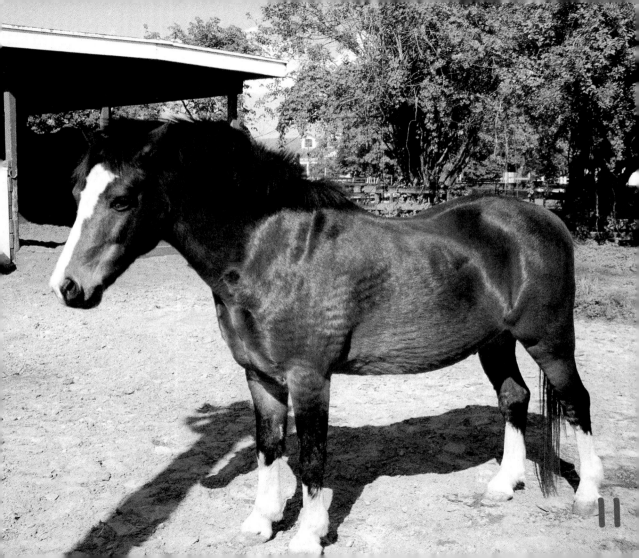

My horses go into the **field** every day.

They like to run around in the field.

13

Horses eat a lot of food.

I feed them **oats** and corn.

15

I **brush** my horses.

Here I am brushing Coco.

Brushing keeps his **coat shiny** and healthy.

17

My horses live in a **stall**.

I must keep their stall clean.

18

My horses go inside their stall at the end of the day.

Good-bye, Star!

Good-bye, Coco!

New Words

brush (**brush**) to rub using a brush

coat (**koht**) a horse's fur

colt (**kolt**) a young horse

field (**feeld**) a place where animals run

mare (**mair**) a mother horse

oats (**ohtz**) a kind of food horses eat

shiny (**shy**-nee) having a lot of shine

stall (**stahl**) a place for an animal in a barn

To Find Out More

Books

Going To a Horse Farm
by Shirley Kerby James
Charlesbridge Publishing

Horses (A First Discovery Book)
by Henri Galeron
Scholastic

Horses and Ponies
by Sandy Ransford
Barron's Educational Series

Web Sites
Kid's Farm
http://www.kidsfarm.com/horses.htm
You can find out what horses eat and hear the sounds they make.

Horsefun Home Page
http://www.horsefun.com/index.html
You can learn some fun horse facts and solve horse puzzles.

Index

About the Author
Heather Miller lives in Cambridge, Massachusetts, with her son, Jasper. She is a graduate student at Harvard University.

Reading Consultants
Kris Flynn, Coordinator, Small School District Literacy, The San Diego County Office of Education

Shelly Forys, Certified Reading Recovery Specialist, W.J. Zahnow Elementary School, Waterloo, IL

Peggy McNamara, Professor, Bank Street College of Education, Reading and Literacy Program